The Book Of Children
Grandma's Words of Wisdom
By
Pat Cher

Illustrations Sonya Robinson

Dear Grandma,

Is it true God loves
me? I don't understand.
Me

Dear Little One,

That's how I think of
you as my dear little one
(You're not so little
anymore, I know). Yes,
God made you. He made
you because he loves you

so very much.

\   Think of someone you love; your Mom, Dad, your dog. God loves you much more than you could ever love anyone. God is Love. Awesome isn't it?

I love you too, but I can't beat God at loving, that's what He is and what He does.

He loves you bigger than the sky, bigger than the stars, bigger than the whole world.

He loves me that much
too.

Lots of Love,
     Grandma

Dear Grandma,

What does it mean to
have a strong or a weak
character?

Dear Little One,

That's a very good
question, and I remember
wondering about that too,
as I was growing up.
Character has to do with
spirit, and how you react
to people and situations.

You might want to think
of it as trying to do
things in the right way.
Just as there are people
who are stronger than
others, so there are
people who are stronger
in doing things that are
right.
For example, it's
sometimes easier to lie
than to tell the truth,
but the strong person
tells the truth.
If you want to have a

strong character you
have to practice being
strong in difficult
situations. Just as a
person who wants to get
strong in body has to
exercise and keep active.

Love you so much,
Grandma

Dear Grandma,
How do I become a kind
person?
Me

Dear Little One,
You are kind already, but
if you want to become
kinder, practice doing
something kind every day.
The more you practice
the better you become at
it.
Love you,
Grandma

Dear Grandma,

How do I talk to God?
Does he talk back? What
do I say when I talk to
Him?

Me

Dear Little One,
    You can talk to God in
any way you want. You
can talk out loud or just
in your heart. You can
talk to Him when you're

alone or when you're in a
crowd. You can talk to
him about anything;
about your friends, about
what makes you happy,
about what makes you
sad, about what you did
today or about what you
want to do tomorrow.
It's easy to talk to God.
Yes, He does answer, but
you have to listen. He
answers in different
ways. He can answer in
your heart, or you can

find the answer in the things or people around you.
Listening to God takes practice, because we can't see him, and we sometimes don't wait or don't look for his answer. I've been practicing for a long time and I'm still not very good at listening to Him.

Love you, Grandma

Dear Grandma,
     What's a soul? Do I
have one? What does it
look like?
     Me

Dear Little One,
     Everyone has a soul.
God lovingly made it in
the palm of His hand.
Awesome, isn't it?
     We can't see our souls
just as we can't see God.
Our souls were made
more beautiful than

anything we know and it's
our job to keep them
beautiful. Every time we
are unkind or unloving our
soul gets a little smear
or a spot (at least that's
the way I picture it).

When someone hurts
you, you also get a spot.
You can imagine how
spotty your soul can get.
Isn't that sad? But, God
is so good that if you tell
Him you're sorry, he'll
make it new again.

The spots someone
threw at you (when they
hurt you) go away when
you forgive them. Sounds
easy, doesn't it?
Remember God loves you
It doesn't matter what
you do, He's ready to
make your soul as
beautiful as it was on the
day He made it.

You're special to me,
Grandma

Dear Grandma,

Why do people get old?
What does it feel like?
Me

Dear Little One,

I once was told that
growing old was a gift, a
priviledge. Not everyone
is chosen to grow old.
Growing old means
becoming an elder.

When you become an
elder you pass on what
you know to others just
like I'm trying to do for
you.
Some people pass on
special skills, others pass
on knowledge.
It's important to those
growing up that they
have someone to teach
them, someone to turn to,
when they don't have all
the answers.
Imagine if you had to

learn everything by
yourself with no help.

Love you forever,
Grandma

Dear Grandma,
    Why do people have
to die?

                    Me

Dear Little One,
    People die when their
time here is finished. It
could happen anytime to
anyone. It is a
frightening thought isn't
it? But, it doesn't have to
be. We have to thank
God every day for the
time He has given us

here, and we have to try
to spend that time
wisely.

God is so much wiser
than we are. He loves us
so very much too. When
we die we get to see Him
and it is only then that
we realise how much He
loves us.
Dying is like going to
another world, going on a
trip. We become more
like God. We see all our
friends and relative who

haven't died, but they don't see us until it's their turn to join God's heavenly kingdom.
His world is much more beautiful than what we have here. There is no pain, no suffering and everyone is kind and gentle. It's a very good and safe place.

Hugs and kisses,
Grandma

Dear Grandma,
My friend really hurt my
feelings. What should I
do?
Me

Dear Little One,
You must be very sad. A
friend can hurt us so
much more than someone
else. Remember what I
told you about
forgiveness. You have to
forgive your friend so
you'll feel right inside.

Those spots on your soul
always make you feel
uncomfortable. Forgiving
is not easy. You have to
ask God who is awesome
and your great friend to
help you. He'll help make
the friendship right again,
if you ask Him.

God is so happy when
you're loving. It reminds
me of the story of the
butterfly. I often think
that when we do the
ordinary things in life, we

are like the caterpillar
and still loved by God,
but that when we do
something with love, in
God's eyes we soar like
butterflies but
butterflies more brilliant
and beautiful than we
can imagine.
Try to be a butterfly
every day.

You are special to me and
to God,
Grandma

Dear Grandma,

What do I do when
people make me angry?
                    Me

Dear Little One,

You have to forgive them.
Your questions remind me
of when I'm driving down
the street and someone
cuts me off or drives
dangerously. I really feel

like calling them all kinds of names. Instead, I remember that God loves them too and I say a prayer for them. I feel tricky doing that because I think that the devil enjoys seeing me angry. It's fun to do the opposite of what he wants me to do.

Love always,
Grandma

3
1
4
2
6
5
7
8
9
10

Dear Grandma,
    How do you be a
friend?
          Me

Dear Little One,
    Friends make life so
much more interesting.
You're asking me a very
good question. It tells me
you already know friends
are important. Always
remember that people
(friends) are much more
important than things.

I have to tell you a true story about someone I know. He has a very special friend. They have known each other since they were in baby carriages. They have not always lived close to each other but they have always kept in touch.

Now both live close by and they call each other at least twice a day. They do volunteer work together. Their friendship has lasted their whole life so far. Imagine that?

How have they done this? They argue a lot. Neither one hesitates about telling the other off. I think the important thing is that they don't hold a grudge. If one of them is mad over something by the time they talk to each other the next day it's forgotten. They forgive and then it's gone.

They are also there
for each other if either
needs help in anyway.

I hope you can find a
friend like that or even
two or three. Friends are
so important.

To be a true friend
you have to follow God's
example. He's always
there when you need Him.
If you want to be a
friend you have to be
there for that person
when it feels good and

when it doesn't feel so
good. In a difficult
situation when you're not
sure of what to do you
can always ask yourself,
what would God do?

You're special to me,
Grandma

Dear Grandma,

My friend is very sad.

What should I do?
Me

Dear Little One,

When our friends are
sad it makes us sad too.
Don't be afraid to show
your friend that you feel
his pain. If you can, do
little things, special
things that show you
care. It could be sharing
a special treat, doing a

favour or standing by
your friend in a difficult
moment.
　　Sometimes it helps if
you just touch the other
person on the shoulder or
on the hand, just a little
touch to show that you
are there for them.
Sometimes a loving touch
can do wonders. Try it
you'll see.
The best kind of friend is
the one who tries to help
you when you are sad.

Love you tender,
Grandma

Dear Grandma,
    My friend does so
many things better than
me. How can I be better?
Me

Dear Little One,
    There will always be
someone who will be
better than you at
something. What you
have to do is find out
what you are very good
at doing.
    Here's something to

help you. When you were born the angels thanked God for you. They knew that God had made you a perfect fit to everyone you would meet. Try to discover that secret.

How? It takes a lifetime for most people. Every night this week, before you go to bed, ask your angel or God to show you one of your gifts.

Also, thank God often

for having made you. Say,
"Thank you, God, for
making me special in your
eyes."
   He did make you
special. You are the apple
of His eyes. Make sure
you also thank God for
your friend. Treasure
your friend because to
have a friend is very
special.
Love you every day,
Grandma

Dear Grandma,
    I'm having problems with a bully. What can i do?
                    Me

Dear Little One,
    First, I will pray for you and for the person who is being a bully. I would like you to pray about it too. Ask God to show you what you must do. Pray that God will change his heart. I think

the bully must be a very unhappy person. Maybe he wants everyone else to be unhappy too.

Secondly, I want you to remember a very important truth. People only have as much power (control) as you and others are willing to give them. What does that mean to you in this situation? The bully is trying to control you by making you afraid. Every

time you show you are
afraid, he wins. Bullies
pick on those weaker
than they are, people
they can control. Now the
difficult part... How do
you break the control he
has over you? Here are
some suggestions.
-Don't show you're afraid,
turn and walk away.
-Find friends to hang
around with maybe others
who are being picked on.
There is strength in

numbers.
-Have special activities in your group. Maybe bully will want to join. Only let him join on the condition that the bullying stops. If they continue, don't let him be part of the group.
-Form a secret society with one or two very good friends, try to find something good about the bully, compliment him about it. When he isn't bullying try to find ways

of being nice to him.
-Talk to an adult, a
teacher, your parents, a
friend's parents, an uncle
or an aunt, someone you
like and trust) about your
problems and see if
together you can come up
with a solution.

Love you lots,
Grandma

Dear Grandma,

My teacher asked me a question today, and I didn't tell her the truth. I told a lie. What should I do?

Me

Dear Little One,

   You must feel sad. I know you don't make a habit of lying. Do you know why most people

lie? They lie mostly
because they are afraid.
So I think that maybe
you were afraid to tell
your teacher the truth.
If you told the truth,
what do you think would
have happened? Now
think about it another
way. If your teacher
discovers that you told a
lie. How will you feel?
It's the same as telling a
friend a lie. Once, they
know you lied, it's

difficult for them to
trust you again.

I know you are brave,
and don't need to tell a
lie. You are also brave
enough to go tell your
teacher you lied. You
don't have to do it in
front of the class, just
ask the teacher if you
can see her at recess or
after class. Remember, to
say you're sorry. The
lying not only hurt you, it

hurt your teacher too.

Here's something a wise man once said:

You know what it's like when you find out a friend is a liar? Whatever he says, after that, sounds false, however true it may be." --Jean Giraudoux

Remember, if you lie one time, it's much easier to lie a second time and then it could become a habit. The other thing about a lie, we sometimes have to lie again to keep it going, and it takes a good memory to remember all the lies. Mark Twain said it best; "If you tell the truth, you don't have to remember anything."

So today I'll say a little prayer for you. As for you, be sure to ask

God to help you do the
right thing, I'm sure that
with such a powerful
friend you'll know just
what to do.

Love you very much,

Grandma

Thank you for reading The Book of

Children, I hope you, your children,

grandchildren enjoyed it,

If you've enjoyed the book, please

write a comment. Positive feedback

helps me keep writing. Leave

reviews on Amazon...

http://goo.gl/ZtsMxD

Note: The illustrations in the book

and the book cover are by Sonya

Robinson

Pat Cher, author
Mi'kmaq Song on
Amazon at …
http://goo.gl/JhQB7B